Dodo Provocateur

ANITA PATI

THE **RIALTO**

Anita Pati was born and grew up in an English northern seaside town. She now lives in London where she has worked variously as a library assistant and a journalist. She has been a Jerwood/Arvon mentee, one of the Poetry Trust's Aldeburgh 8, won the *Wasafiri* New Writing Prize and was a winner of the inaugural Women Poets' Prize. *Dodo Provocateur* is her debut pamphlet and won *The Rialto*'s second Open Pamphlet Competition.

*

Whether cataloguing a species' slow demise or a child's stirrings in the womb, *Dodo Provocateur* is an exuberant box of treats, full of life and linguistic gusto. Flipping effortlessly between distant colonial horizons and the house next door, Anita Pati is a real original: a poet whose wry humour and slant perspectives on the world don't fail to surprise and delight.

Sarah Howe

In *Dodo Provocateur,* Anita Pati's voice has emerged as original, provocative and restlessly reflexive. Addressing themes and subject matter ranging from childhood memories to extinction, racism, Jimmy Savile and the Pendle witches, the expression is crisp and striking and each poem partakes of a lexical virtuosity that echoes Fran Lock, Geraldine Clarkson and Imtiaz Dharker. These poems are not satisfied and they quietly push the boundaries.

Steve Ely

Anita Pati's poems sound entirely her own. Every line in *Dodo Provocateur* brims with music and meaning. These playful poems explore racism and patriarchy in Britain – a land of Shepherd's Pie, Shakespeare, *Kwik Save* and crime scenes – via an astonishing range of characters and forms. But in this least auspicious of places, Pati still manages to winkle out reasons for hope. We are lucky to have such 'knuckly flowers'; such 'beetley treasure'.

Clare Pollard

for Ishy

ACKNOWLEDGEMENTS

Many thanks to the editors of the following magazines and anthologies where several of these poems first appeared: *Ambit, Butcher's Dog, Live Canon 154 Sonnets, Magma, New Statesman, Poetry London, Poetry Review, The Best British Poetry, and The Rialto.*

Much gratitude to these organisations/schemes: The Jerwood/Arvon Mentoring Programme, The Poetry Trust, The Rebecca Swift Foundation, *The Rialto, Wasafiri.*

Thank you to the tutors/mentors who over the years have commented on some of these poems: Steve Ely, John Glenday, Daljit Nagra, Clare Pollard, Peter Sansom, Warsan Shire, Jackie Wills and Tamar Yoseloff.

Thank you also for feedback from excellent and generous workshop groups, particularly at the Poetry School; for encouragement and advice from non-poetry and poetry friends; to family; and to *The Rialto* team including Michael, Nick, judge Richard, and to my editor Rishi. To my mentor Kathryn Maris for believing in my work from the start, and especially to Dan, Alex and Ishy. x

First published in 2019.

The Rialto c/o 74 Britannia Road, Norwich NR1 4HS, United Kingdom

ISBN 9781909632097

Typeset in Berling 10 on 12.5pt
Design by Starfish, Norwich
Printed in England by Page Bros, Norwich, Norfolk
Cover illustration by Rina Banerjee

CONTENTS

ORNITHOLOGY

Some bards know
the plume
in their chest from the nest.

Others follow and fuss,
fusing domes from quartzy moss,
swelling the flock with voice.

For those too wounded to squawk:
earth tamps down their song.

SILVER JUBILEE

She runs red crayon
around her bunched fingers
to draw knuckly flowers.

A bouquet of fists –
a family grabs hands –
limbs clash in colours:

English maypole blues,
skin pinks,
a celebratory pageant on paper.

Her face, hushed,
is a copper ha'penny,
serene, like the Queen's,

when the brick gets in,
sailing like boats
she'd learned to fold as a toddler

to land square at her face
(kaleidoscoping
the patio glass)

from where their splinterous
GET BACK HOME! whoops
ransack the air. And no,

it's not fair that no-one will see
her picture now.
Should she draw it again?

PAPERDOLLS OR WHERE ARE MY CURLY SCROLLS OF SISTERS?

They are wedging me open with lapwings, the feathers
angled and birded to hurt. But I've a tight heart.

Dad took the call, uprooted the brood to bacon barmcakes.
Here we're tiny, a fistful of morula, massing.

A leper sold us salted cucumber in newspaper twists
then slipped drainwards, *that's where you come from*

your hands are dirty, sssshhhh shut your mouth while you eat
said the mynah bird, no, said the settlers.

Mum escaped through airmail script to slinky heat.
That upfaced tooth extracts its roots; such a mossy cliff.

The cliff is crocheted pearl, gnatty whirlpools, round ligaments.
Where are my larvic, volcanic sisters?

I'd crouch in the boiler room, making ski lifts from off Blue Peter.
If we'd stayed I'd have been the biggest family,

you're so quiet we thought you'd disappeared: sssshhhh
cut me a row of paperdoll aunties –

keep cutting inside me with your instruments. You are making holes
for light to get in. I'll stay in Recovery if you nurse me.

Where are my mockingbirds for sisters?
Tetra Pak houses, rainy terraces, grey, no laughters.

I've threaded the mothers on daisy chains which I pluck
some times. Plant in oasis.

Turmeric lightens the skin: we've become cream boaters and lace.
Fold up your plaits, village girl. I know I lapse; please keep trying.

'TWIXT
(after Shakespeare's Sonnet XXVIII)

Call this love? I'm whacked and dainty over u –
that pigeon heart has pestered me all year.
You Twitter in my ears a mating coo
and digitise your *Rati* everywhere.
My brain's not a computer yet it fires
a trillion cross-wired pings that sting of thee.
And when I work to block you out, my screen
spurts Facebook feeds that eat the nub of me.
I pick your pixelled face to breathe hard on,
I flatter flesh but then your steaming head
spirals into kitty snarls so I
start furrowing your golden forum threads.
I meditate I plead I flick you off
and still you grunt in me no mind to stop.

THE GIRL WHO WOULD BE KING

Is it English streets are paved with gold,
Papa? Where chaps sport bowler hats
to hide their rice for dinner?

Guess no one wears *chappals* but Tower Jewel heels
that soar to heaven, and their feet don't pickle?

Bet there's no hullabaloos over pilfered *mooli*
or rapscallion cockroaches to flaunt bottoms at me.
Plus no antsy pantsy.

May I squat in a red telephone box
and pray to Dr Who?

They're not all bloody bastards like you say,
Papa, you nincompoop!

Mr Kipling will give me a French Fancy
then croon:

Roxanne, you pretty princess.

But I will call myself Joanna
and eat jackfruit jelly with Eton litter.

Policemen will give me fishunchips
or clips on the ear.

This is the fair play in England, says Mr Mishra.

What the Dickens, Papa, will they think of me,
Graham Greene and HG Wells and
those noble and free
                          like the Queen?

When we go to live there and shoo their monkeys
off their ruddy faces, they might thank us?

BAGA TWO

That Arab spring sprung on me
each Tuesday night at Windy Harbour
boys' school gym. The red leotard Mum
put me in to get my BAGA four and three.
Forward rolls, fig rolls, Kwik Save
on the drives back home, horse vaulting
onto tacky floors, and cabbage loos where she,
the girl with mousy plaits, would corner me.

'Why did Cadbury's dip you in chocolate?'
(And who the flip was Chalky?)
Till one day: joy! I saw her hands quail
back into her cardy sleeves.
'Why've you only three fingers?' I asked.
She never narked me after that.

HER WORLD IS FURY

Her as a pockled crab, hidden in shingle.
Her as spat-on sprat, slivered
bilged back in the Caspian sea.
Scuffed knees: Hers:
half-orange pitted skins:
calloused: Her bullet caps.

The slashed arms of Her: oil leaks
plunging through seawater.
Her voice, a whistle in the Wadi desert.
Her with the brown flower hands.
Her eyes a kingfisher's fanfare.
The belly of Her, sometimes crossfire.
Her eggs, drowsy bulleyes.

When Her puzzles, Her
wrinkles dance green
in the heart monitor. And
Her hair trawls the nine worlds
birthed in a Nordic night. But the heart
of Her is bruise waiting bee-sting.
Her, whose soul tails lost swifts on the upwinds.
Her, whose wrath comes in thunder's four-second delay.

EARWIG KID

For three years,
the kid skipped
school to flip earwigs

from the wall
to the gravel, dangled earwigs from

their pincers. He'd mass piles of beetley treasure
in his game of Solitaire

or peer beneath their bellies
checking if the brain was there.
Stray, hopeless kid with frizz in his hair.

Earwig ankles wriggling in air!

He'd see earwigs polished like prefect brogues,
nipping out the damp bits from Year Eight and Nine kids,
laying eggs in furred ears, puttering in crevices

the kid imagined lurking in every rotted thing. One rascal morning
at the hockey fields, a team of giant earwigs   sidejigged out of crackened turf.
Tall as gutted lime trees,   they span   black ballerinas
hooking up the villagers by their fleecy perms,   squirting amber gland scent
at two-legged predators,

You! You! Did you look at my hair?

MAL

Them dogs won't touch us three.
On Pendle Hill, no wind can whip us,
no brack of clouds from Chorley pall us.

Look. Dogs here are bogbounce happy,
kiddies snuffing balls and whatnot near Malkin,
families tripping from the corrugated towns.

They skirl around me, my own dog Whistler:
springer spaniels, border collies,
Sunday walkers flush-cheeked fed.

Proud marchers in their slimy wellies,
clodding soft black puddings underfoot.
We're all white sons, Joe, my white son.

But they're checking out my army kecks,
peering at the tail prickling stiff
and scared between Whistler's legs –

a chastise stick pointing at me, malefick, like
it's my fault I smack them. But both muck around.
I'll bat painted witches when they shrink from my hands.

I'll rag Joe's mum till her mess washes off in Bowland drizzle.
These valleys, the shutdown towns: Nelson, Bacup,
their streetlights slag us slant like toothless whores.

Those dark moors wither when we're near,
their split mills fallen now warp foreign
blackamoors in Burnley, Blackburn, Padiham.

I'll flick them all: cotton grass under my thumb,
their spirits sporing across the Pennines
floating to a halt at my dog's mangy jaws.

OPERATION HOMEGROWN 2024:
MY LONE WOLF HAS BOARDED

Hello, Hamid, we have you
     frisked in white noise, a marvel
for spooks.

     Tap on to the bus
and there you are, my Bollywood star ☺
startling CCTV screens.

Chipped to the pips in your wrist
     you pulse like a pacemaker
jerking the hearts of passengers.

See – they lovingly claw
their kids tight from you:
fans terror sick
on the 30 to Hackney Wick.

Fighter!
We've watched you:
playground spats; Twitter raps;
rancid degree from a revamped poly.

We've caught your sexlife with your exwife:
your sperm swim safe in tubes at our labs.

SKIRRRUP/
              /switch screens
and we've got you
six foot four, now limping.

Let us finger your unzipped spine
                        till it spills
a marshbog of sleeper cells; somatic green.
Your lung, what a wheezy kameez!

Messiah!
Holiday out there? +cardiac failure+
Tasered, you could be our man.

                  *

The fall from the sky,
severed thighs, travel guides – your flash whites –
we'll crash you lot to the ground.

Martyr, are ya? That golden screen beckons.
Oh Hamid, honey, how could you?

SELF-PORTRAIT EXAGGERATING MY UNKNOWN FEATURES

(after Adrian Piper's Self-Portrait Exaggerating My Negroid Features, 1981)

Romping from the Sundarbans to Wimbledon,

roaming eye patched under pelt, plum lip, blood iris,

my hennaed hands bare Shellac™ nails, trained to scratch

your judging mouth. My unmapped features will not shut up.

So flatten my ribs – coral under your divers' feet –

here's my East End Ghee belly fleeing controlling pants.

Enough of my nose (it knows) and man will it scent you out,

sliced onto the Scoville scale of vehemence.

Yet times my war calls vapourise once hitting air;

I sweat behind skin-lightening Hollywood mango cream.

And when black curls sprout from your wooden, straight, blonde floors,

you'll swipe the roots to find peroxide gritting there.

And so you know my made-up face? I make me up.

I'll echo me, I'll echo us, we won't shut up.

OLGA'S SHOULDERS

Too fat
for her loculus
lies Olga Nobikov,
whose creambloat shoulders
perplexed Victorian funeral directors
in the catacombs of Kensal Rise cemetery.
That body! How could they squeeze *pirozhki* in,
her noble belly rolls of dumplings
straining the leading of
the coffin, Olga's
décolletage
boned in
but
bursting?
'O
your
Doric
arches,'
tremors proud
husband Septimus,
'will, turned to pearls, pronounce our
love immaculate!' They diced her ribs, this
Russian dish, like stuffing in an English
mince-and-nutmeg cold water crust pie.
And so she lies, safe from the robbers,
primed for afterlife, in cryptic
majesty, the trophy wife.

THE TALE OF WILBUR'S VICTORIAN SEWAGE PUMPS

The two-barrelled Prince Consort engine
designed by a colonel named St John,
was fantasised fondly in Hitchin.

Colonel St John had pondered
how sewage, to fuel one onward,
like money, should never be squandered.

Conceived over parlour-time Horlicks,
cream-splashed Imperial promise
twirled ostrich eggs, rare hot-house relics.

And if he was right in his thesis,
Lloyds would fund the long leases
to sieve those Victorian faeces.

Water in furnaces blasted,
cylinder, syringe and masthead,
industry maketh the bastard!

Now India flamed Wilbur's fire –
breathless he swore he would try her,
flying the flag for the Empire.

…to scoop those moist paddy bellies
…to palm sticky bosoms on date trees
…to snatch from a land of tan coolies

Piston, condenser and fly-wheel,
pump rod and slip shaft in Leeds steel,
Blighty Almighty at his heel!

Though Myrtle his bone-brittled wife said,
pleading each night in their thin bed:
"Darling, it's better in Guildford,"

Wilbur had gaped in the Black Hole:
Maharajah was his role.
He'd failed to notice the peril –

liquidity's safer than solids.
Will fell, malarial, squalid,
with sunstroke pinking his forehead.

Sewage is no match for rubies.
Wilbur St John never knew this
and sank, one more victim of hubris.

Now fantasies fabled in Hitchin,
once home to the two-barrelled engine,
power the ghost of dear St John.

I, WASHERWOMAN

"As bulls enraged, or lions smear'd with gore,
His bands sweep wide o'er Goa's purpled shore."
                          from The Lusiad OR the Discovery of India
                          Luís Vaz de Camões

This viceroy with the smolten nose
like whittled *swede*   ✦
marches through the gallery of gilded men.
          It's Dom Felipe whose crucifix of bone
swings high!   And blood dust rises.

Men sail from Lisbon to our Old Goa town,
clammy as they topple curs that bask by pink mansions;
trample damsel frangipani.

Thanks *Master* for garlands that choke my neck.
I don't want your Jesus but I'll strip for you
and wash your linens, Dom Felipe.

Under pickerel sky you watch me squat
a copper pot by the temple. Yes
I'll make sheets gleam like toddlers' teeth.

When the wildcat prowls the sewer by night
          at the perimeter fence
and the guards snooze off their cashew feni,
he comes to me in blackened robes, sceptre flash.

A gecko clamps in its jaws a moth
whose purple wings breathe a twitch like velvet gills.

(His gowns they mute the bell in my ribs.)

Gecko hiccups the moth-knot down
which warps beneath its calloused trunk.
Master tucks flowers behind my ear.

JANIS JOPLIN ROBS MY DRINK

which isn't normally bourbon
but tonight my throat is
a tangle of stringhoppers
and she's swimming up my oesophagus
with red-rimmed irises
from all that crying
and a flailing breaststroke
that thumps my heart.
Up, into my mouth
she sings her ball and chain
swinging her urchin hair into my ears.
And I'm reaching for the whisky
and tumbling it through her
again and again.

THERE BUT FOR THE GRACE OF JIM

He was a titchy boy, unthumpy
               cowered on Jimmy's sofa.
The kind of child you'd squash against a surgical screen
or stuff in scrubs and slither under
a hospital trolley. Freckled perhaps

and also, though I was 7, I saw a fellow fearer.

Would he meet Santa or Kenny Dalglish
or dithered in Savile's aura, was he fixed?

Choose me Jimmy, from out the TV.
But I wasn't blond or scrawny or lost enough.

Where are you now, boy, still twitchy?
fiddling for lads to be 'King' for the day or
meet the muppets or Gary?

Or maybe wheeled off already
dead on your twinkling trolley.
That ribbon around your neck;
Jim fixed it for you, not me. I'm sorry.

CRIME SCENE
i.m MH

I never knew of you,
neighbour,
until the leaflet
pushed through my door
that said *MURDER*.

For seventeen years
we shared our estate,
must have unlooked
an eye-lock –
we all do that here.

Your home's hollowed out
but for clowns
in white masks:
forensics, mimetic,
green-gowned,

fingering crimes with tapes,
your last life (us silent).
Now you're dead
can I wish I'd known you
for all that time.

THE OLD HIGH-RISE BELL-BOY

There have been toilets made here
of this lift, where some may reach
to the sky. He wipes cuckoo froth spit
from the button that says *floor three*
and presses a finger as if in his navel,
watches the steel-skinned ceiling spin.
Budgie's safe in the flat quizzing mirrors,
tracking the Soviet probe. He, he rallies
on racing tips, antacid drinks, doorstep toast.
He's patrolling Dakota Mansions today,
a grade up from Dagenham House.
'Chip off the old tower block!' Yes, he wants
to badinage with you. Look! On floor seven,
blanched madams with pugs in bags will coo
in his carriage. On gold-spiked pumps,
on cigarette stubs, they'll swing on his tales
of rent and cramps. And make him a crown
from chicken bones. And blow him kisses
through sequined moans. He'll *stand clear
the doors are closing*, but none will get in.
No more than maximum load ten persons
can ring this puddle of piss. *Floor ten!* Alarm
bells sound. Our boy will see the light,
float above the lift shaft, nailed to the next flight.

THE GOOD NEIGHBOUR

Maureen hobbles towards me this streetside.
Her neck like broken.

Her slippers slap but her head sleeps.
Her lot was taken.

And her white hands are soft
bread fingers.

And she seems to shiver a lot.
Hot strangers.

Pudding bowl hair from Pine Day Centre.
Moss in mouth.

She wears that quilted jacket again.
Let me out!

'Do you have 10p for a cup of tea?'
T to Tar you.

'They can f-off. Will they hurt me?'
F to Feather you.

They'll plop those pennies onto your eyes.
But you won't be queen.

And stake your wishbone as the prize –
oh, Maureen.

'Will you always help me?'
Her line.

In her window; an amber silhouette
facing mine.

PUB LUNCH
i.m Norman Prowse Williams

We'd shouldered him from the nursing home,
wheelchair griping in the boot, and him,
dressed in his smartest pants, legs like spoons.
At the Greyhound Inn, I'd knocked his knees,
those China bowls, on the table edge
and though the pain shuddered him,
he rolled his eyes, quipped his jokes.
But how he ate – shepherd's pie,
the wilted salad spurned for meat.
And when it was just him and me,
I couldn't look; the mash, the peas,
his quivering hands, the arm that once
had ripped a tree from its roots
faltering with a knife. He knew I knew and
I couldn't look when his right wrist shook
from the weight of a fork. And still
he brushed crumbs from his Gabardine suit
watched the addled families. *Such a treat*
to be taken out, he said. *Thank you for taking me out.*
After the half Guinness, apple pie, cream,
I asked, have you finished, Dad? Are you done?

BLACK HOLES AND STARS
for D

You, little man, are calling me but I don't know how to get in.
You invite me upstairs where the floorboards creak.
Cranks coil through your head. At your ears there are uncracked panes
and the rain pecks the glass from the sea-sky.
RUN from the fog bowl of wool being tipped.

When your torso writhes it axles my gut. I know, kid, it hurts
and I can't throw cherry blossom over your hair to bless you
or I can. But it won't work, like it did, once, stranded in the dunes
at Freshfield pines. How to scrape salt packed in your eyes?
Or shift buckthorn mugging your fisted heart?

Once, aged three, you quizzed me on God. I would skewer
the ones that harmed you this way. Fat night smothers you,
your father breaks. Where do you sing in that Buddha-shaved head?
Keep me close, don't disappear when you tell of the messenger,
the billions of years that, crystalled, harrow within you.

*The universe is only black holes and stars; I was the sun and now
I'm a black hole leeching from life.* A fallen dunlin
worries soft at my palm; smooth your wings, tread the sand.
We'll squat in the sun's trickly eye, don't take flight
yet, I'll beat for you, keep here.

AN UNBORN CHILD WONDERS IF IT'S WORTH IT

They say the seas catfight by night,
that rabbling gales scorch huddled girls?
Well, toffee, Haiti howls, that's right.

Lizards and ladies stoned in deserts,
rows of heads popped by rocks in red little shocks?
Oh, poppet, the tongue that cocks will cop it.

And grannies and mice are vial mummies in cold countries,
mummies in others suck gun through their gums?
The choice, Lucy Locket, is yours to grace this earth.

Liver, cornea, lymph rotted from rust in water,
babies burping the expiration of suicide daddies?
Every little helps through WaterAid monthly, kiddo.

But the tremor of stars stirs furious lovers together?
Yes. Points and counterpoints horrify me.

And the migratory Brahminy kites swoon at Lake Chilika?
Pumpkin, most folk are wanting to flee.

Maybe I'll whistle to see who picks up my tune?
Weigh it up, petal, maybe we'll see you soon.

DODO PROVOCATEUR

Europeans hunted you mercilessly,

because you beakies wouldn't be doves or albatross.

Those whitish irises probably grotted and balled and seized,

black undertail coverts jutting at strumpet-starved sailors,

marooned on Mauritius, exotic, just not Bideford, Perth or Poole.

Why gobble pebbles big as nutmegs to temper your guts,

and prove fresh meat for rusky sailors, declaring you foul?

'Belly and breast pleasant enough in flavour,' they said.

If only they'd waited a few decades later before they snuffed you

forever, for being cloven-footed, turkey! You know,

you and your bulging brethren could have been common as peacocks,

not stuffed through your hooks in old Copenhagen or folded in sketchbooks.

Mauritian Martha, who froze your fruity body in gin?

Now of the Marthas exists only bitty skin, you pigeons.

NOTES

'twixt was commissioned by *Live Cannon* to respond to Shakespeare's Sonnet XXVIII for *154 Sonnets* (2016). *Paperdolls or Where Are My Curly Scrolls of Sisters?* was commissioned for *Poetry London* in response to artwork at the APT Gallery, London.

The Girl Who Would Be King: the poem references Rudyard Kipling's story *The Man Who Would Be King.*

BAGA Two: BAGA stands for British Amateur Gymnastics Association which set gymnastic awards (BAGA awards) at different levels of proficiency.

'Chalky White' was a racist 'comedy' standup character in 1970s' and '80s' popular culture.

Dodo Provocateur: Research from Errol Fuller's *Extinct Birds.*

*

Cover image: Rina Banerjee
Dodo bird and her Extinction met Dutch sailors in the Indian Ocean while they were looking for fortune and existence both plain and simple sailed into new worlds and paradises or experience death was one notion, 2014
Acrylic and ink on paper
32 1/4 x 24 inches
Collection: Ford Foundation
Image: Courtesy of the artist Rina Banerjee and Galerie Nathalie Obadia, Paris/Bruxelles